T0069055

TORTURE
AND THE WAR ON TERROR

THE FRENCH LIST

tzvetan todorov

TORTURE
AND THE WAR ON TERROR

TRANSLATED BY GILA WALKER

WITH PHOTOGRAPHS BY RYAN LOBO

Seagull
BOOKS

LONDON NEW YORK CALCUTTA

Seagull Books 2009

Original text © Tzvetan Todorov 2009
English translation © Gila Walker 2009
Photographs © Ryan Lobo 2009
This compilation © Seagull Books 2009

First published in English by Seagull Books, 2009

ISBN-13   978 1 9064 9 736 1

British Library Cataloguing-in-Publication Data
A catalogue record for this book is available
from the British Library

Typeset and designed by Sunandini Banerjee, Seagull Books
Printed at CDC Printers Pvt Ltd, Calcutta

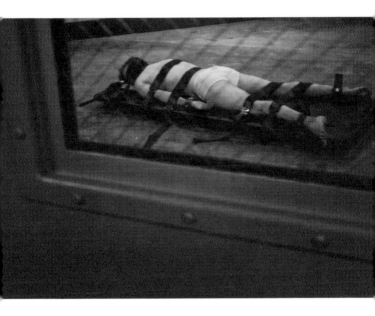

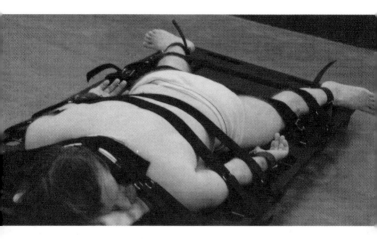

Since the beginning of this new millennium, it has become common practice to speak of the 'war against terrorism' as a new world war. The consequences of this choice of words are demonstrated in the politics adopted since '9/11' not only by the US but also by several European governments.

There are a number of negative ramifications to using such a phrase, as former president George W. Bush did to describe the current situation. I will start by examining some of the usual criticisms that this phraseology has attracted before giving some cautionary advice about the consequences.

First, it is clearly a metaphorical war that we are waging, as in the 'war against poverty' or the 'war against drugs', in the sense that, unlike a traditional war, it is not a human opponent that is being fought but, rather, a scourge that may never be completely removed. This loaded metaphor risks inducing other unwanted consequences. As Carl von Clausewitz famously maintained, war has the same objectives as politics but, at the same time, it represents the negation of politics—since all interaction is reduced to a test of military strength. War brings death and destruction, not only to the adversary but also to one's own side, and without distinguishing between guilty and innocent. Winning a military victory does not mean winning over a people to one's cause. This was the lesson of the Versailles Treaty in 1919, the Battle of Algiers in 1957 and the occupation of Baghdad at the beginning of this century. A war against terrorism or against evil presents the dual disadvantage of being unlimited in time and space: such a war may never end and the enemy remains an unidentified abstraction that can manifest itself anywhere.

The term terrorist also suffers from a lack of specificity. It simply informs us that a person or an organization does not act in the name of a state, and that it indiscriminately attacks civilians, soldiers, buildings and means of transport. But it tells us nothing of the global objective pursued by these militants or of their particular motivations.

The absence of any indication as to the reasons for
their combat is not fortuitous, of course. Identifying
them by their action alone hinders the development
of empathy and, *a fortiori*, of sympathy for these individuals. The people who fought for independence
in Algeria and against apartheid in South Africa
were described as 'terrorists' for the same reason. Yet
such a designation is of no help in fighting them;
to know an enemy, it is not enough to name the
weapons it uses. Even if restricted to Islamic terrorists, the term remains overly vague since it does not
allow us to distinguish, for example, between
Chechens and Palestinians fighting for their country's independence and international terrorists affil-
iated with Al-Qaeda who pretend to fight for the
defeat of the crusaders and the victory of Islam. And
the fact is, not taking into account these widely dif-
fering motivations makes it all the more difficult to

influence the networks of sympathizers that alone ensure the persistence of terrorism.

To speak of this fight as a 'war' also risks leading to questionable strategic choices. Whereas wars are fought with missiles and bombs, the war against terrorism requires other means altogether. If investments are focused on weaponry, there is a risk that resources will be lacking for an in-depth study of the adversary. In 2006, only six out of a staff of a thousand in the American Embassy in Baghdad spoke Arabic fluently. American soldiers often have the impression that the Iraqis understand only the language of force and yet they themselves speak not a word of Arabic.

Internally, the damage can be just as serious. The declaration of a state of war makes it possible to suspend civil liberties and guarantees and to reinforce executive over legislative power, not to mention the Manichaean education inflicted on one's own population. Any criticism of government policy is perceived as undermining troop morale, even as a betrayal of one's country . . . when freedom of speech should be one of the most treasured gifts of democracy. The effects of a 'war against terrorism' are particularly dangerous because the war may never come to an end and so the suspension of law could continue indefinitely.

One of the most detrimental consequences of this situation is the damage done to the status of truth in a country's public life. On numerous occasions, the US government has deemed truth a negligible factor that can be easily sacrificed to the will for power. We now know that the preparation for and outbreak of the war against Iraq was based on a double lie or double illusion—namely, that Al-Qaeda was connected to the Iraqi government and that Iraq possessed weapons of mass destruction, nuclear, biological or chemical. This casual attitude toward the truth did not disappear even after the fall of Baghdad. Just as the entire world was discovering the pictures of torture and the stories of executions at the Abu-Ghraib prison, the American government was asserting that democracy had gained ground in Iraq. And while hundreds of prisoners rotted away in Guantánamo, detained for years, subjected to degrading treatment, without lawful judgement or the possibility of defending themselves, the US government nonetheless proclaimed that its forces were engaged in the pursuit of human rights.

These developments are cause for concern precisely because they are taking place in the world's first democracy, not in a country subjected to a totalitarian dictatorship or to a repressive traditional regime. Despite party pluralism and freedom of the press, apparently it is possible to convince the population of a liberal democracy that the truth is false and that falsehoods are true. Those responsible for this situation are, in the first place, the institutions where public opinion is forged: the government, the major television networks and the newspapers. With political action increasingly reduced to political communication, the majority of the population has let itself be carried away by fear. To protect one's own life, ensure the safety of one's own people and eliminate threats considered imminent, the usual legal and moral precautions have been discarded. Verifying and assessing information, reasoning and arguing are now seen as indicators of a lack of courage and sense of responsibility.

It is not only in terms of military efficiency that such a strategy remains questionable; reducing

international relations to the 'friend–enemy' alternative is hardly a means of guaranteeing victory for the ideal that one is out to defend. Supposing it were possible to eliminate the carriers of evil—what benefit would there be in it if we ourselves have to become evil to do this? This is the age-old dilemma inherent in the idea of war for the sake of a higher good. To bring the Christian religion to the Indians, which teaches equality and love of one's neighbour, the conquistadores subjugated them through war and showed them nothing but hate and contempt. Christian morality's reputation was not enhanced through this adventure.

To bring the virtues of Western civilization and the values of liberty, equality and fraternity to the Africans, the European colonizers waged war on them; they imposed an external order upon the vanquished, granted themselves the right to command them and showed disdain for their personal dignity. Civilization did not shine through this adventure either. During the Second World War, massive air bombings of civilian populations by the Germans aroused indignation because it illustrated once again the Manichaean logic that sees everyone on the other side as guilty. Then came the day when the Allies had recourse to the same tactics under the guise of breaking German resistance, and barbarism crept a little further into the world.

Moreover, it is not unusual to see recipients of a violent shock respond to it with even greater violence. Experiments conducted by psychologists have shown that human beings tend to react to an aggression with a higher degree of aggression, because the harm that people undergo always seems greater to them than the harm that they inflict upon others. Illustrations of this amplification are easy to find in history. Hitler feared the Bolshevik threat, not without reason, but the means he used to neutralize it turned out to be a cure worse than the disease, even for the German population. During the Sétif demonstration in Algeria in May 1945, over 100 French citizens were massacred. The colonial power responded by a repression that led to the killing of between 1,500 and 45,000 Algerians, depending on the source, which means between 15 and 450 Algerians were killed in retribution for every French citizen. The bombs dropped on Hiroshima and Nagasaki punished the Japanese for their militaristic policy and the countless cruelties they had perpetrated in the war in Asia, but they nonetheless constituted a war crime of a magnitude never before seen. In several Latin American countries, the danger of a *coup d'état* from the extreme left was averted at the cost of a military dictatorship, which, ultimately, was responsible for 30,000 'disappeared' opponents in Argentina, 35,000 confirmed cases of torture in Chile and the abandonment of the most elementary democratic principles elsewhere.

At the beginning of the twenty-first century, the attacks against the Twin Towers in New York caused the death of approximately 3,000 people. By 2007, four years of war in Iraq, started on the pretext of punishing those associated with the attack (entirely unfounded, let us not forget), had caused the death of a considerably higher number of Iraqis, estimated at between 60,000 (by *Iraq Body Count*) and 600,000 (by the medical journal *The Lancet*), which means between 20 and 200 Iraqis for each American killed. Seeing enemies everywhere eventually led to a deplorable escalation in the means chosen to fight them. In answer to the torture practised by one side came blind attacks committed

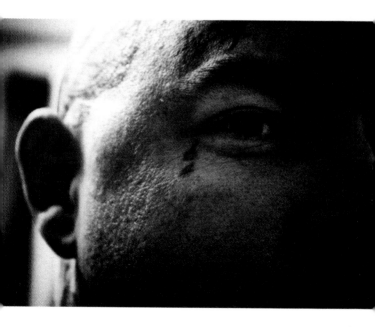

by feeble-minded, manipulated individuals and children trained to kill and to die—and vice versa. Where will the barbarism end? Is bombing someone you consider an enemy more, or less, civilized than slitting the person's throat?

It is highly doubtful that we can impose good by force. International relations seem governed less by the idea that 'the end justifies the means' than by the fact that 'the means outweigh the ends'. The US government and a few of its allies have been trying to bring certain political values to the Middle East by occupying and subjugating Iraq. Yet the long history of relations with this part of the world suggests to Arab and Muslim populations that this is once again merely a pretext and a cover-up; that the West is, in fact, only interested in controlling oil resources or setting up military bases. Subjugating a country after bombing it, killing thousands, leaving tens of thousands homeless, practising arbitrary imprisonment, brutality and torture, are simply ways of exporting 'Western values' that compromise them permanently.

There is, however, another much more efficient way of spreading the values one holds dear, and that is to proclaim them loudly and embody them fully. Ideas and principles have formidable power. This is illustrated by the many changes of regime in a given state. Governments always have greater military and police force than the few rebels who defy them. But in the eyes of a good part of the population, the latter stand for an ideal of liberty and justice and represent the promise of a happier, more dignified life. The rising tide of a popular uprising can overpower the brute force of the rulers. When these values are exported, they help the weak triumph over the strong. This is what happened during decolonization in the twentieth century—a process that was often driven by 'Western' ideas of freedom and equality that had been turned against Western colonial powers. Unfortunately, professional advocates of war tend to underestimate the power of ideas and values.

Nothing illustrates the damages of an unlimited fight against 'the enemy' better than the adoption of torture as a legitimate practice, which is what ensued in the aftermath of '9/11'.

Such acts of torture are found in history since antiquity. There is nothing animalistic about them. One can even observe a reinforcement of this practice with the growing affirmation of our human identity. Elements related to acts of torture can be discerned in the behaviour of primates, but only human beings have pushed to such an extreme the consciousness of the other's consciousness, the ability to imagine what the other imagines. To deliberately inflict suffering on a being like oneself, one must be able to put oneself mentally in their shoes—a capacity more developed in human beings than in any other species.

Over time, torture became so omnipresent that attempts were made to outlaw it. In European countries, torture was prohibited in the course of the eighteenth century and the Universal Declaration of Human Rights proscribed it throughout the world in 1948. This prohibition was specified and codified by the Geneva Conventions in 1949 and solemnly confirmed by the United Nations Convention Against Torture in 1984, covering torture and 'other acts of cruel, inhuman or degrading treatment or punishment'. These documents defined torture as acts 'inflicting severe pain or suffering', be it physical or mental. The signatures on these

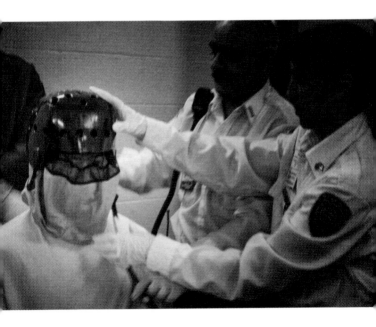

conventions have not prevented the governments of a number of countries from resorting to torture whenever they deem necessary. They have done their best, however, to conceal such practices and publicly deny their existence. Consequently, any such prohibition has not been strictly respected. Acts of barbarism have not vanished as if by magic. But an ideal of civilization has been established that exerts an effect of moderation and strongly diminishes the number of violent acts inflicted. The novelty of the current situation resides in the fact that the US government itself proclaimed the need for torture. This breach has made torture into a subject of public debate, with people calmly arguing for or against it.

The decisive turning point was the so-called 'Torture Memo' submitted by the US Department of Justice's Office of Legal Counsel on 1 August 2002.[1] Written in response to increased protest against the use of torture on prisoners by agents of the US government, and to the threat of criminal proceedings against interrogators, the memorandum cites legal reasons according to which the acts committed are deemed lawful and do not fall into the category of prohibited acts of torture as defined by international conventions and the US Code (§ 2340–2340A).

The strategy of the document is to admit to the acts of violence endured by the prisoners, but also to contest their qualification as 'torture' in what amounts to a redefinition of a term that did not seem problematical until then. According to the Memo, 'certain acts may be cruel, inhuman, or degrading, but still not produce pain and suffering

---

1 See, for example, Dana Priest, 'Justice Dept. Memo Says "Torture" May Be Justified', *Washington Post* (13 June 2004). For the full text of the 'Torture Memo'—'Re: Standards of Conduct for Interrogation under 18 U.S.C. 2340–2340A'—please visit www.washingtonpost.com/wp-srv/nation/documents/dojinterrogationmemo20020801.pdf

of the requisite intensity' to be qualified as torture. For an act to constitute torture,

> [. . .] it must inflict pain that is difficult to endure. Physical pain amounting to torture must be equivalent in intensity to the pain accompanying serious physical injury, such as organ failure, impairment of bodily function, or even death. For purely mental pain or suffering to amount to torture [. . .], it must result in significant psychological harm of significant duration, e.g., lasting for months or even years.

According to the Memo, sensory deprivation, a widely used technique in prisoner interrogations, does not fall into the category of torture: 'while many of these techniques may amount to cruel, inhuman and degrading treatment, they do not produce pain or suffering of the necessary intensity to meet the definition of torture.'

To be sure, this document did not introduce acts of torture, but, by making them legal, it contributed to their spread. From then on, it was commonplace to see and hear commentators in the US media overtly defending the use of torture (even publishing articles with catchy titles such as 'It Works!'), with no further concern as to legal justifications. Several Republican presidential candidates for the 2008 election declared they were in favour of torture. The subject also entered the arena of academic discussion, with renowned professors providing legal, political and moral arguments in its favour. The condemnation of torture was no longer self-evident; it became a question on which opinions diverged and the subject of publications bearing titles such as *The Torture Debate in America*.[2] The next

---

2 Karen J. Greenberg (ed.), *The Torture Debate in America* (New York: Cambridge University Press, 2006).

thing we know, we'll be seeing chairs and depart-
ments established to teach the whys and hows of
torture . . .

A distinction should be made between the
attitude of torture apologists in the media or in
universities and that of official representatives of the
government who refuse to admit that such acts are
committed on US territory. This is precisely why
the 'forceful interrogations' of prisoners take place
outside the US: in the jails of allied countries
(Abu-Ghraib, Iraq, or Bagram, Afghanistan), in
CIA's secret prisons or in US military bases in
Kosovo (supposedly) and Guantánamo. That
Guantánamo is situated in Cuba, a country known
for its human rights violations, is a sinister irony.
Thanks to these external locations, the US can
freely infringe upon these same rights. Apparently,
according to a Council of Europe report, suspects

have also been imprisoned and tortured in secret prisons set up in Poland and Romania.[3]

For the same reason, the US government invented a brand new legal category of 'illegal enemy combatants'. Generally, perpetrators of violent acts are clearly divided into two groups that, when arrested, are subject to different laws but that still possess certain rights. In peacetime, they are criminals, protected in any state that abides by the rule of law through what is called *habeas corpus*, defended by attorneys, and judged in accordance with traditional law. In wartime, they are enemy soldiers who, in case of capture, must be treated according to international conventions. In what category do Al-Qaeda terrorists fall? They are not regular army

---

3 Council of Europe, Committee on Legal Affairs and Human Rights, 'Secret Detentions and Illegal Transfers of Detainees involving Council of Europe Member States: Second Report'. Available at: assembly.coe.int/CommitteeDocs/2007/EMarty_20070608_NoEmbargo.pdf

members of a country that signed the Geneva Conventions, so they cannot benefit from those protections. Do they fall into the category of ordinary criminals? Here is where the expression 'war against terrorism' proves particularly useful. Because we are dealing with a 'war', the laws applicable in times of peace do not apply. Yet, since the war is not directed against another country, the international conventions do not apply either! And since this 'war' has no end in sight, the government that declares war sets itself above national laws and international norms for an indefinite period of time. The 'illegal enemy combatants' category allowed the US government to place apprehended individuals outside the reach of laws and norms, and hence to practise torture.

The 'Torture Memo' maintains that the acts under question do not fall into the category of torture. For them to be deemed torture, it suggests, as we have seen, there must be a loss of a leg or an arm, the inability to stand up, a burst liver, incontinence for life—even death, as the Memo states, without any hint of irony. Inflicting suffering on people close to the prisoner, like his wife or children, does not amount to torture since there is no loss of a vital organ. As for mental suffering, it must be permanent—it can be defined as torture only retrospectively, if the mental disorder does not go away after several years. In all other cases, there will have been no torture and the US will have respected the international conventions.

Let me remind the reader in a few words of the kind of treatments inflicted on prisoners that 'do not amount to torture', as reported in the international press. In prisons scattered throughout countries outside the US, the detainees have been regularly raped, hung from hooks, immersed in

water, burned, attached to electrodes, deprived of food, water or medicine, attacked by dogs, and beaten until their bones are broken. On military bases or on US territory, they have been subjected to sensory deprivation and to other violent sensory treatments—forced to wear headphones so they cannot hear, hoods so they cannot see, surgical masks to keep them from smelling and thick gloves that interfere with the sense of touch. They have been subjected to nonstop 'white noise' or to the irregular alternation of deafening noise and total silence; prevented from sleeping, either by the use of bright lights or by being subjected to interrogations that can last 20 hours on end, 48 days in a row; and taken from extreme cold to extreme heat and vice versa. None of these methods cause 'the impairment of bodily function' but they are known to cause the rapid destruction of personal identity.

Lastly, let me add that the leaders of the European Union cannot consider that their own responsibility is not implicated in the torture that is more or less overtly acknowledged by the US government. The secret services of their countries have actively collaborated with their American counterparts, delivering information and contacts that lead to arrests and hence eventually to torture. Such practices, even though they have been proven, have not elicited the slightest official condemnation from the French, British or Spanish governments, and the fact is that silence implies consent. To be sure, their reluctance in this regard is understandable: these allies—be they in Europe, Asia or the Americas—depend on the US for their security. Hence they do not have the moral right to condemn methods while at the same time they benefit from their results. And governments are not the only ones that have responsibility in this matter. Insofar as you, I, and other citizens of these countries do not speak up against torture, we become accomplices to its continued use.

People are often, and justifiably, outraged that innocent people may have been tortured. It is important to recognize that, in a number of cases, the people who have been subjected to torture are guilty of various crimes or criminal intentions and that some of them have, in fact, killed or planned to kill. Just as for the death penalty, such cases must be our starting point if we want to oppose torture.

To address the justifications provided for acts of torture, we must start by setting aside the false claims of the 'Torture Memo'. The reasoning of the Memo—paradoxically so, for a legal document prepared by competent jurists—proceeds from a form of magical thinking insofar as it pretends that we can act on things by changing their name. It is not because we say that the systematic destruction of a person will not be *called* torture that it ceases to *be* torture. Common usage and international conventions would designate such practices as belonging to the category of torture; thus reality is not altered in any way by this new designation.

We need to focus not so much on the legal texts as on the arguments set forward by advocates of such practices, which reflect and shape the thinking of political decision-makers. The most commonly encountered argument is based on what is known in the US as the 'ticking bomb' scenario, which was popularized by the TV series '24': a terrorist has been arrested who has planted a bomb. You know it will explode in an hour, but you don't know where it is. Will you allow thousands of people to die in the explosion (hundreds of thousands in the

case of a nuclear bomb!) because you refuse to torture one person? If you answer 'no', you are more or less conceding that torture is admissible, even commendable in certain cases. All that remains to be done, from this point on, is to calculate the gains and the losses. Thus to save even a single irreplaceable and invaluable human life, it becomes legitimate to torture—especially if the person is a 'bad guy'.

In actual fact, this case arises frequently only in arguments in favour of torture, not in the real world. It requires the conjunction of so many conditions that the situation becomes highly improbable: you have to know that there is a bomb; when it will explode; who planted it; find him/her in time; conceal the capture from his/her accomplices so that they don't move the bomb; get a truthful confession right away, and so on. A great scenario for a thriller, or for the study of utilitarian morality in first-year philosophy classes! It is an evocative moral dilemma, but one that in no way corresponds to observable torture as it is practised. During the Algerian War, the French army arrested anyone who appeared suspect for whatever reason, and not those who were known to have planted a bomb. They tortured suspects to find out who their enemies were and where they were hiding.

So let us leave aside this hypothetical scenario and examine the actual practice of torture. Torture is used in particular when an army is facing a guerrilla force. The aim is to collect information about an enemy that could not be found otherwise, since often one doesn't know who is the enemy and who is not. In fact, one of the main reasons given for torture is that we are dealing with a particularly savage war unlike any other and with an enemy so horrible that, if it wins, we are in danger of losing

our most precious possessions. The only way of defeating it is by using, in turn, illegal means.

This is more or less the position that the President of the United States of America overtly defended, in response to criticism of CIA interrogation practices, when he declared, 'the American people expect us to find out information, actionable intelligence, so we can help them, help protect them. That's our job.'[4]

We may consider it inhuman and degrading to enter into such a debate, as if human beings did not share an intuitive understanding that torture is inadmissible. But since the subject has become an open debate, we shall accept this temporarily in order to argue within its framework.

4 See, for example, John Byrne, 'CIA Still Operates "Black Sites" Overseas, Senior Counterterrorism Official Says', *The Raw Story* (5 October 2007). Available at: rawstory.com/news/2007/CIA_still_operating_black_sites_overseas_1005.html

Every aspect of this demonstration can be challenged. First, nothing proves that the information obtained under torture is true. Philosophers throughout Western history, including Aristotle, Beccaria, Montaigne and Hobbes, have noted that confessions (or the lack thereof) tell us much about the resistance capacities of the tortured individual but that the information thus obtained is not very dependable. The innumerable confessions—all products of the imagination—obtained during the witchcraft trials in the sixteenth century are proof of this. There was, it has been noted, a particularly high number of confessions in Germany—not because the devil felt more at home there, but because the methods of torture were crueller.

Let us examine the argument in the terms in which it is situated. Torture, it is basically said, is necessary to win the war: this justification is utility.

But the actual results leave much to be desired. The example of the French war in Algeria is telling in this respect. Torture was practised by the army to fight terrorist attacks. It helped the French army to dismantle some Front de Libération Nationale (FLN) networks and to win the Battle of Algiers, but it also caused France, indirectly, to lose the war. The reports of torture reinforced solidarity in the Muslim population. For each fighter arrested, several new ones stood up, determined to take revenge, and the portion of the indigenous population that had been neutral until then joined the opposition. Moreover, hostility to the war in metropolitan France was primarily motivated by these same reports. In turn, international public opinion and governments in several influential countries began siding with the Algerian independence movement. With French determination to maintain the rule of law now challenged, they could no longer see the cause as just.

The illegal means used by the US government to fight terrorists have diminished neither their number nor their violence. To the contrary, those methods have become an argument for recruiting new jihadists who are even more dangerous—they know they risk torture if taken prisoner and so they chose to die as 'kamikazes'. At the same time, the meagre benefits obtained through forceful interrogations at Abu-Ghraib were reduced to nothing by the collapse of the US's moral standing. What was supposed to contribute to a final victory made it more remote still; because, to win that war, the government had to win over the sympathy of entire populations in Muslim countries, and this is hard to do when you have earned the reputation of a torturer.

The 'utilitarian' argument fails to justify torture. Is it possible that the people who cite it have not noticed this? This is hard to imagine. Then there must be a different reason motivating it, a reason more difficult to admit in public or, even, simply to oneself. In fact, it is expressed in clear terms in the stated goal of 'terrorizing terrorists'. Since the latter have caused so much dreadful harm—killing innocent people, spreading fear everywhere and threatening our most cherished values—we must exact our revenge and make them suffer as much as we have, if not more. We must show them that our democratic values have not weakened our ability to be tough. It is a matter of symbolically repairing the past by inflicting comparable harm upon them (*lex talionis*), thus assuring they will know what to expect in the future. When we terrorize terrorists, we indicate our willingness to become their image

in the mirror and to be even more determined as terrorists than they have been.

It is this need to punish the agents of evil that accounts for the persistence of torture throughout history. This is the real reason for the torture acknowledged by the US government and the broader reason for the support mustered among its citizens to engage in the Iraq War and to embark on a generalized 'war on terrorism'. These can be explained, not so much by the legal arguments propounded or by a need to defend the principles of democracy and the advances of Western civilization, as by the fear that gripped the leadership of the country, which was then communicated to its citizens. The threat of death, real or imaginary, led to the conclusion that 'everything is permissible'.

The choice of torture as a form of retributive terror also brings inner satisfaction to those who practice it, even if they have difficulty admitting it. After being wounded and humiliated by an aggression, they can in turn humiliate their aggressors and thereby restore their own self-esteem. As one former soldier in the Algerian War explained 40 years after the events, 'There was a certain form of jubilation that could be felt in watching such extreme scenes [. . .] Doing with a body what you feel like doing to it . . .'.[5] Reducing the other to a state of utter powerlessness gives you a sense of limitless power. This feeling is obtained more from torture than from murder; because, once dead, the other is an inert object that can no longer yield the jubilation that comes from wholly defeating the will of the other. On the other hand, raping a woman in front

---

5 See Tzvetan Todorov, 'Torture in the Algerian War', *South Central Review*, 24(1) (Spring 2007): 18–26. Translated from the French by Arthur Denner.

of her husband, parents and children or torturing a child in front of his father yields an illusion of omnipotence and a sense of absolute sovereignty. Transgressing human laws thus makes you feel close to the gods.

These feelings are not the prerogative of a few isolated sadists; they are felt by a great many individuals but only in the exceptional circumstances of war—which is another reason not to interpret the fight against terrorism as a war, as a situation in which legal norms are suspended. It is not true that war reveals what exists beforehand: it creates something new. To understand the desire to torture, rape and humiliate does not require a hypothetical 'torture instinct' (or 'death instinct'); such a desire derives from the same source as our other desires, but it takes this violent form when, as in war, other paths of social recognition are blocked.

It is time to leave the utilitarian framework, which we have entered for the purposes of argument. Torture is not only to be condemned because it does not yield the results that we are expecting. Above all, it is unjustifiable because it is an inadmissible attack on the very idea of humanity. It is the surest indication of the barbaric, of the extreme of human behaviour that makes us reject the humanity of the other. Once again, torture is more telling in this regard than murder: in torturing someone, I do not content myself with getting rid of the person that bothers me; I derive satisfaction from the victim's suffering, from excluding this person from the pale of humankind, and this enjoyment continues as long as the person remains alive. Torture leaves an indelible mark—not only on the victim but also on the torturer.

Institutionalized torture is even worse than individual torture because it subverts the very foundation of the idea of justice and law. If the state it-self becomes the torturer, how can we believe in the civil order that it claims to bring or to sanction? Legal torture extends the scope of the destructive action that it exerts. Instead of stopping with the torturer and the victim, it spreads to all members of society, since they know that it is being practised in their name and yet they avert their eyes and do nothing to put an end to it. As a rule, citizens in liberal democracies will condemn without hesitation the violent practices of a state that tolerates torture, especially of a state that systematizes its use, as in the case of totalitarian regimes. Now we have discovered that these same democracies can adopt totalitarian attitudes without changing their overall structure. This cancer does not eat away at a single individual; its metastases are found in people who thought they had eradicated it in others and considered themselves immune. This is why we cannot

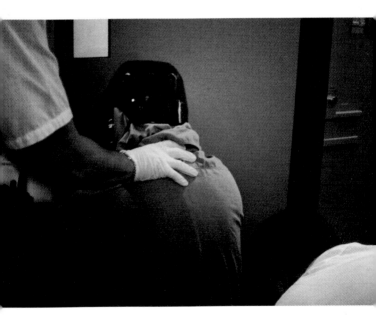

be reassured. Our countries can vanquish external enemies but they must remain wary of themselves and of the mutilations they risk inflicting upon themselves. And it is incumbent upon all of us to prevent such mutilation.

AFTERWORD

This essay was written in 2008 before Barack Obama was elected President of the United States of America. His presidency may mark a break in US foreign policy, thereby rendering some of my comments obsolete. I have opted to leave them as is for several reasons. For one thing, the expected changes may not occur; if they do, they may concern certain countries and not others. A second more fundamental reason has to do with the fact that the infringements of democratic principles discussed in this essay occurred in an indisputably democratic state. For this reason, they illustrate a danger threatening democracies in general. What happened once can happen again. These pages should no longer be read as a critique of the existing situation, but, rather, as a warning, based on one page in contemporary history, against a possible reaction to dangers, real or imaginary.

March 2009

ABOUT THE PHOTOGRAPHS

These photographs were taken at Oak Park Heights Prison in Minnesota in 2005 during the making of a documentary film, and with the support and permission of the institutional staff. The Minnesota Correctional Facility—Oak Park Heights, 5329 Osgood Avenue North, Stillwater, Minnesota 55082-1117, opened in 1982, and receives those offenders from other adult male institutions who are classified as 'maximum custody' or 'extreme risks to the public'. The level five, maximum-security institution has a population of 436 (January 2009). These photographs do not include any non-American prisoners or any terrorism suspects and have nothing to do with the war on terror. The photographer does not necessarily share any or some of the views of the writer, and his photographs have been used as an accompaniment to the essay's general area of concern and not to illustrate any specific example or case. The image of the man strapped to the board were taken during filming; the videographer was prevented from shooting this event on video. According to the prison authorities, he was strapped to the board to prevent him doing injury to himself or others.

Ryan Lobo
June 2009